"Some educators believe that up to 80% of what a child learns during the school year can be lost after 48 hours . . ."

Dear Parent,

Picking up this book shows that you are interested in your child's reading abilities, and that you have accepted the challenge of working with your child during a time when education may take a back seat to other adventures.

Summer is the perfect time to reinforce reading skills taught during the school year. Some educators believe that up to 80% of what a child learns can be lost after 48 hours if not reinforced aggressively and consistently. Think of what 12 weeks away from school will do!

Summer Bridge Reading Activities is designed to help children have fun while maintaining and extending reading skills while away from school. Each workbook consists of a variety of stories and poems which review reading skills from the grade the child is leaving, and previews skills which will be introduced in the upcoming year. *Summer Bridge Reading Activities* builds reading confidence, making the transition to the new school year easier. Phonemic awareness and controlled vocabularies are used to reinforce word recognition, contractions, compound words, recognizing details, and sequencing.

This summer, take an active interest in your child's education. Even though school books and homework are set aside, and curfews may be extended, it is important to remember that you as a parent are the most important teacher your child will ever have, and that it is necessary to challenge your child's mind even when school bells are silent.

Happy Summer Learning!

George Starks
Creative Director

Table of Contents

Remember that it is always a good idea to read the stories more than once. This builds good reading skills, fluency and comprehension. You may want to spend more than 1 or 2 days on the stories and follow-up activities!

Parent Tips

Beginning and young readers have a lot to learn about what reading is and how it works. Letters, sounds, associations, and word recognition are all new concepts and may be a bit overwhelming at times. With reassurance, patience, and willingness to help your child overcome their insecurities, their learning experience and love of reading will be drastically heightened. Summer is the perfect time to develop your parent-child reading relationship!

1. Fill a paper bag or shoe box with letters of the alphabet or simple words. Have your child draw them out one at a time. They keep the ones they know, and put the ones back that they don't know. After drawing all the letters or words, review the ones they do not know before putting them back into the bag or box. Add variety to this activity by using a timer to see how many they can solve in a certain amount of time.

2. Write letters on index cards and place them on a table. Choose one such as C and say "CAT." Have your child choose another letter such as R, and have them make up their own word using the ending you used. Example- you say "CAT" they say "RAT." Use a variety of words, and even make up your own.

3. Use alphabet cards to make simple words for your child. Leave off a letter, say the word, and have your child find the missing letter and place it where it needs to go to complete the word you originally chose.

4. Find some wooden cubes and write letters on each side with a marker. Place the cubes in a plastic cup, shake it, and toss them on a table, floor, or any flat surface. Ask your child to make words out of the letters which are showing.

5. Give your child index cards and have them write the words they are studying on, one card at a time, then have them draw a picture to go with the letter they wrote. Play the memory game where you turn all the cards over and take turns trying to match the word with the picture.

6. Write words on index cards and place them in a paper bag. Have your child draw them out, one at a time, and say the words. When they have several out of the bag, see if they can make a sentence with the words. They do not need to use all the words, just the words needed to make a complete sentence.

7. Have your child do daily reading related activities working with words they have not yet mastered. Keep the words they know in a separate "BRAG," or "I CAN DO STACK." Add words to this stack as they master them. This helps them take pride in how well they are doing.

8. Read a story "to" your child, then take turns reading the story "with" your child. You read a line, then have them read the line after you. Alternate for the entire story.

Learning to read is like learning to ride a bicycle! Practice makes perfect!

Summer Reading List
2nd to 3rd Grade

Why Mosquitoes Buzz in People's Ears,
Aardema

Who Sank the Boat,
Allen

Mr. Popper's Penguins,
Atwater

Animals Should Definitely Not Wear Clothing,
Barrett

Beware of Boys,
Blundell

The World That Jack Built,
Brown

Hooray for the Golly Sisters! (and others),
Byars

The Great Kapok Tree (and others),
Cherry

The Lucky Baseball Bat (and others),
Christopher

Miss Rumphius,
Cooney

Aunt Eater's Mystery Vacation,
Cushman

James and the Giant Peach (and others),
Dahl

Pigs in Hiding,
Dubanevich

Hattie and the Fox,
Fox

Emily and the Enchanted Frog,
Griffith

My Place in Space,
Hirst

My Great-Aunt Arizona,
Houston

Alfie Gets in First,
Hughes

Mama, Do You Love Me?,
Joose

Here Comes the Strikeout,
Kessler

Soap Soup,
Kuskin

Henrietta's First Winter,
Lewis

Little Blue and Little Yellow,
Lionni,

Owl At Home,
Lobel

In a Cabin In a Wood,
McNally

If You Give a Moose a Muffin,
Numeroff

Old Enough for Magic,
Pickett

Elizabeth and Larry,
Sadler

There is a Carrot in My Ear (and others),
Schwartz

The Mud Flat Olympics (and others),
Stevenson,

The Widow's Broom (and others),
Van Allsburg,

The Boxcar Children (series),
Warne

The Napping House,
Wood

Bird Watch,
Yolen

Summer Reading
Contract & Calendar

My parents and I decided that if I complete my Summer Bridge Reading Activities book and read _____ minutes per day, for 20 days, my reward or incentive will be _____

Child's Signature_____ Parent's Signature_____

Jorgie's Jive

You can do it! I'll be helping you along the way! Summer Reading is fun and helps you grow!

Day	Book	Minutes	Parent Initials	Day	Book	Minutes	Parent Initials
1				11			
2				12			
3				13			
4				14			
5				15			
6				16			
7				17			
8				18			
9				19			
10				20			

Jake And The Pet Store

Jake wanted a pet but he didn't know what kind of pet to get. He went to the pet store at the mall. He walked up to the man in the pet store and said, "I'm here to get a pet."

The pet store owner replied, "You have come to the right place and you can choose from the many pets we have." "What kind do you want?"

Jake said, "I'm not exactly sure, so maybe we can just look for awhile." Jake saw a little black and white spotted puppy that seemed very friendly. He saw a calico cat that was playing with a ball of yarn. He watched goldfish blowing bubbles in the fish tank. He laughed at the little white mouse running around on its exercise wheel. He covered the sleepy gerbils with sawdust.

Well, thought Jake, I like friendly animals and clean animals. I love fish that can swim and blow bubbles at the same time. I love watching animals run, as well as quiet animals that sleep.

"What will it be?" asked the pet store owner.

Jake replied, "They are all my favorite. I can't decide, so, I guess I'll just have to have them all!" "Where will you keep them all, asked the pet store owner?" Jake laughed and said, "In my bedroom of course!"

Follow up activities for "Jake and the Pet Store"

Reading Comprehension questions for discussion with child and parent/adult:

1. What kind of a person do you think Jake was?
2. How much money do you think it would take to buy the animals Jake wants?
3. If his mom says that he can buy only one, which one should he buy and why?
4. Where would he put them all in his bedroom?
5. Do you think the animals will be happy there? Why or why not?

Match the animals with the correct action!

spotted puppy	blowing bubbles
white mouse	sleepy
gold fish	friendly
calico cat	running around
gerbils	playing

Add word endings such as "ing," "s," "ed" to the words listed below. There are five words that you cannot add "ed" to. Why?

spot	clean
swim	cover
run	blow
sleep	choose

Fill in the blanks.

1. The Calico Cat is _____ with a ball of yarn.   play, plays, playing, played
2. The little white mouse likes to _____ to get exercise.   run, runs, running
3. Gerbils like to _____.   sleeping, sleep, sleeps
4. The goldfish are _____ and blowing bubbles.   swim, swims, swimming
5. The _____ puppy is friendly.   spot, spots, spotted

WRITING PROMPT: Make a list of other animals that might be in a pet store. Choose an animal in the story or one of your choice and write a story about the animal. Sound spelling in acceptable.

My Home

My home has many rooms used by many people. In the kitchen we all eat together. Mom is there a lot. Our family room is a room where we can watch television or play on the computer after our homework is finished.

The living room is a place to visit when company comes or a place to read quietly. Dad loves to read the paper there at night when he comes home from work.

My sister says that her bedroom is "off limits". We boys are not to go in it when she's not there and only when she tells us to come in. She says, "It's my own private place."

My dad and mom's bedroom is kind of like that. We usually knock or call out if we want to talk to mom and dad when they are in their room, unless it is terribly important.

My brother, Allen and I have a bedroom together. We have our toys, games, clothes and bunk beds in there. Lots of times that room gets pretty messy.

I think my private place in my home is the bathroom! Someone usually knocks on the door and tells me that it is their turn for the bathroom, so could I please hurry. Oh, well.

Jorgie's Jive

If you have a stopwatch, you can keep track of how long it takes you to read the story. Each time you read it you could keep track to see how well you're doing!

8

Follow-up Activities for "My Home"

Reading Comprehension questions for discussion with child and parent/adult:

1. What does the word private mean?
2. How do you think the boy in the story feels about sharing a bedroom with his brother?
3. Do you think he should feel that way? Why or why not?
4. What rooms do you think are the most important in a home?
5. What do you think would happen if a new baby sister came to live at this home?

Add a vowel or two to make these words turn into long vowel words. Some vowels will come at the end of the word, some will be in the middle.

Match the room with what you think goes with it.

living room	toys, games, bunk beds, books
sister's bedroom	television, computer, some game
boy's bedroom	chairs, stove, table, refrigerator
kitchen	couch, chairs, rugs, lamps, pictures
family room	a bed, pillows, dolls, off limits sign

1. not _____   2. cap _____
3. kit _____   4. red _____
5. bot _____   6. her _____
7. bet _____   8. ran _____
9. pop _____   10. rod _____
11. hug _____   12. last _____

Write T if the sentence is true, F if it is not true.

1. Dogs and fish like to swim in the water. _____
2. Knives, forks and shovels belong in the kitchen. __
3. Newspapers are red. _____
4. Refrigerators and food go together. _____
5. Sisters and moms are girls. _____
6. Boys, girls, dogs and cats need sleep. _____

WRITING PROMPT: Draw a picture of your home and label the rooms. Write a short description of your house. You could write about your favorite room.

9

The Park

My name is Sammy. In the summer we go to the park often. There is always something to do there. There are swings to swing on and slides to slide on. We can climb on and crawl through the castle. On the outside there is a big curly slide.

The first time I went to the park I was too scared to go on the slide by myself, so my big brother went with me. I go down it all by myself now! I think that it's lots of fun!

The park has two terrific sandpiles. Sometimes I take my toy cars and dump truck with me to play in the sand. I like to build roads and tunnels in the sandpile. I also build houses and mountains too. I love doing this because it is so much fun! When I forget to bring my cars and truck with me, I find rocks and pretend that they are my cars.

The most fun I have ever had was when our family went to the park and flew our kites together. My dad helped me get mine into the air and showed me how to get really high in the sky. It was fantastic! I love going to the park.

Jorgie's Jive

Have you read a good library book lately? There are some good ones listed on the "Summer Reading List!" Remember "sound spelling" is just fine when you are writing your own stories.

Follow-up Activities for "The Park"

Reading Comprehension questions for discussion with child and parent/adult:

1. What things did Sammy and his family see at the park?
2. What other things do you think they might have seen at the park that were not in the story?
3. How old do you think Sammy was in this story?
4. What do you think are some of the reasons why he was too scared to go down the slide at first?
5. What else could Sammy have used in the sandpile when he forget his cars and truck?

Go back to the story and make a list of words from the story that mean more than one. (plurals).

Write a rule for the words listed at the left. Hint: the only one that doesn't follow the rule is the word two. Another word that doesn't follow the rule is "we."

1. _____   2. _____   3. _____

4. _____   5. _____   6. _____

7. _____   8. _____   9. _____

10. _____   11. _____   12. _____

13. _____

Unscramble the letters to finish the sentences.

1. Does being brave mean being _____? unrfadia
2. A _____ is a brave community helper. ffiregtrihe
3. Could doing the _____ thing mean being brave? tgrih
4. We can always call 911 in a real _____. emgeneryc
5. Do you think _____ are brave when they go into space? asnttrauos
6. When I go to the _____ I try to be brave and not cry. tstdien
7. Big dogs _____ me when they come up to me and growl. ecrsa
8. _____ doesn't always mean that you're not being brave. ycingr

WRITING PROMPT: Make a list of things that you used to be afraid of and another list of things that you are afraid of now.

The Library

Behind my door adventures are free,

So open it quietly and come to me.

I am a library and through my door,

Are shelves and shelves of books galore.

Books will take you anywhere,

Look around for books to take you there.

They take you into the sky and to outer space,

Into the ocean, a deep, deep place.

They can take you to white sands,

Or to far away distant lands.

Read the opened books to see,

What the world can really be!

After reading the poem do the following:

What kind of a place is the library?

A. a dark place

B. a small place

C. a place with cupboards

D. a quiet place

How can books take you places?

A. by airplane

B. by ocean-liner

C. by reading with imagination

D. with a travel agency

Distant lands means:

A. anywhere

B. far away places

C. your neighborhood

D. your state

List at least 4 ways to have an adventure through reading.

1.

2.

3.

4.

The Pond in the Jungle

In the jungle there is a small pond. Nearby the pond live many animals. One day a tiger said, "It is so very hot." So he waded into the pond. Two monkeys came along. They said, "We are so hot." They jumped into the pond. "It is hot," said three squirrels. They swung down from a tree branch and dropped into the pond. Wow! One tiger, two monkeys and three squirrels in the pond in the jungle!

Here comes four wild pigs. Listen to what they have to say. They said, "It is just too hot", and they rolled into the pond. "We are hot and sticky," hissed five snakes as they slithered into the pond. Then, six frogs hopped off their log into the pond because they too were hot. Seven lions came along and roared, "The day is too hot for us," so they sprang into the pond.

Goodness me! One tiger, two monkeys, three squirrels, four wild pigs, five snakes, six frogs and seven lions in the pond in the jungle! Eight alligators popped their heads out of the water. They said, "We used to be hot, but now we are not." "We are just hungry, real hungry!" One tiger, two monkeys, three squirrels, four wild pigs, five snakes, six frogs, seven lions, splashed, crashed and sprang from the pond in the jungle! Eight alligators in the pond in the jungle.

Jorgie's Jive

I hope that you are doing the comprehension questions, they are an important part of reading! Are you keeping track of the points you've earned so far?

Follow-Up Activities For "The Pond In The Jungle"

Reading Comprehension questions for discussion with child and parent/adult:

1. What is the difference between a pond, a creek, a stream, an ocean and a puddle?
2. Which animals in the story are probably the strongest, the meanest?
3. Can you name all of the animals that appear in the story?
4. What other jungle animals do you think might live in the jungle?

Verbs are action words. Go through the story and list all the verbs.

Put the correct punctuation at the end of the sentence.

1. My sister and I have a stamp collection
2. The raging storm smashed into our house
3. Does anyone know where my tennis shoes and socks are
4. How many boys and girls were in the bicycle race

Circle the words that are spelled correctly and cross out the misspelled words.

knot	maed	breekfast	pancakes	careful	speel
right	stove	vacation	shoees	spoil	sandwitc
bikeng	undrline	circus	applcake	attention	station
tertles	alligators	crashied	slithered	penmenship	twinkled

WRITING PROMPT: Choose a jungle animal. Pretend that you are that animal. Write what you would do. You could also rewrite the story using different animals.

The Lost Wheel

My name is Larry. I have a little red wagon. I've had it for a long time. It's great because you can put things in it. I like to haul things around the yard like sticks and leaves. Sometimes

I hook it up to my old tricycle and pull it that way. I even take my little brother and sister for rides in it.

"Sorry", say I, no more rides, a wheel came off somewhere and I can't find it anywhere." I looked in our front yard. I looked all over in our back yard and couldn't find it anywhere.

My friend Allie lives next door. I thought that maybe the wheel might have come off over there. We both looked in her yard. I also took my wagon to school with me a while back for "show-n-tell", so I looked in our schoolroom, on the playground and all over the schoolyard.

I asked my friends and family to help me find the wheel but so far, no luck. We looked in our house. Mom looked in the kitchen. Dad looked in his workroom , even in his toolbox. I looked in my bedroom, the living room, the spare room and even the bathroom. My little brother, my little sister and I looked in our toy boxes.

Where else is there to look, I wonder? It's not in the bird cage or the bathtub. I checked out the cat's litter box and the mailbox. The doghouse! The doghouse! Hey, everybody, it was in Skippy's doghouse! Now I wonder how it got in Skippy's doghouse? Just tell us all about it, Skippy.

Jorgie's Jive

I hope that you are having a great summer. Are you reading a great book? Check the summer book list to find one that you like!

Follow-Up Activities for "The Lost Wheel"

Reading Comprehension questions for discussion with child and parent/adult:

1. Name all the places that Larry looked for his lost wheel.
2. Where did his family look for it?
3. What places were the best places for the lost wheel to be? Where else could they have looked?
4. What do you think will happen to the wheel now?
5. What does it mean when the story mentioned the "spare" room? What do you think would be kept in a spare room?

How many pets does Larry's family have? _____
List what they are.

Put a vowel in the blanks to make real words.

s _ nd	cany _ n
dec _ de	_ mpty
dr _ nk	cop _
ch _ nge	bus _ ness
cr _ wd	believ_
bott _ m	g _ rden
gl _ de	_ sland
fl _ at	_ce
f _ nally	h _ rse
f _ int	_ dea
fam _ ly	h_ppen
k _ tchen	j _ in
imp _ rt _ nt	f _ gure
h _ ngry	m _ ment
n _ ise	mill _ on
l _ sten	par _ nt
_ rder	m _ self

Re-read the story and underline all the compound words, then write them down.

1. _____ 2. _____
3. _____ 4. _____
5. _____ 6. _____
7. _____ 8. _____
9. _____ 10. _____
11. _____ 12. _____

WRITING PROMPT: Write what you would do if you had a red wagon. Wagons are pretty tough, write how you think the wheel came off. Where? When?

17

Dreams

I dream almost every night. I wonder if pets ever dream when they are asleep.

My dog, Runner, likes to run all the time. He probably dreams of chasing cats and other dogs. He might even catch a butterfly in his dreams. "Run fast and jump high, Runner!"

My sister's dog, Poly, loves to eat all the time. He probably dreams of finding a buried treasure of dog food. Maybe in his dreams he might dig up a pile of dinosaur bones! That would be quite a find for him. It would take him a long, long, long time to eat a pile of dinosaur bones even in his dreams. "Keep eating, Poly, keep eating."

My cousin's cat, Taci, is always cleaning herself. I wonder if she dreams of having servants to keep her fur soft and shiny all the time. Maybe in her dreams she could invent a special "keep clean, kitty" machine made just for her. "Keep clean, Taci, keep clean!"

Do you think that fish dream of swimming in the sky or that birds dream of flying in the ocean? Could it be that lions dream of having their claws clipped and their teeth brushed? Maybe worms dream of being as big as snakes and snakes dream of running with long spider-like legs. Could monkeys dream of going to school, while children dream of climbing trees and swinging on jungle vines? I wonder.

In my imagination, I can be or do anything without even going to sleep. Do animals have an imagination? I wonder.

Jorgie's Jive

When writing make-believe stories, you are using your imagination! Remember to "sound spell" is writing down each sound you hear in the words.

Follow-Up Activities for "Dreams"

Reading Comprehension questions for discussion with child and parent/adult

1. Do you think animals really do dream? Why or why not?
2. What do cats do to keep themselves clean?
3. What other things might you find in the animals' dreams?
4. What kind of dreams do you have? Which ones are your most favorite and least favorite?

Read these sentences and choose a different word/words to replace those with a line through them.

1. Dogs might dig up a pile of ~~dinosaur~~ bones. _____
2. My dog can run ~~fast~~ and jump ~~high~~! _____and_____
3. Children might dream of climbing ~~trees~~. _____
4. I wonder how it would feel to run on ~~spider-like~~ legs._____
5. Monkeys love to climb ~~trees~~ and swing on ~~vines~~._____,_____
6. Snakes ~~crawl~~ and slither along on their tummies. _____
7. I need to use a ~~net~~ to catch a butterfly. _____
8. Ducks waddle back and forth when they ~~walk~~. _____

Write contractions using these words:

cannot	_____	it will	_____
we are	_____	that is	_____
you will	_____	she is	_____
they are	_____	should not	_____
had not	_____	they will	_____
does not	_____	she will	_____
would not	_____	was not	_____
he is	_____	has not	_____
do not	_____	I will	_____
we will	_____	are not	_____
I am	_____	it is	_____

WRITING PROMPT: Draw a picture of one of your dreams and write about it.

19

Rainbow Rockets versus Space Kickers

Our soccer team, the Rainbow Rockets, had practiced hard all week for the game against the Space Kickers. The coach tells us to practice, practice, practice, be good sports and have fun! "Remember," he says, "use just your feet and heads. The players guarding the goals are the only ones who can use their hands."

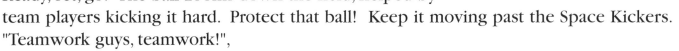

On Saturday, we met on the playing field dressed in our green shirts, blue shorts, shin guards and shoes with cleats. We won the "penny flip" so we got the ball first! Goalies in place by their goals. Kickers are ready. Blockers are on alert. Everyone is in the right spot. Ready, set, go! The ball zooms down the field, helped by team players kicking it hard. Protect that ball! Keep it moving past the Space Kickers. "Teamwork guys, teamwork!", shouted our coach. The ball was kicked to Jeff, Jeff kicked it to Ben, Ben to Spencer, Spencer to Flip, Flip to Scooter! Blocked by a Space Kicker player! Saved by Mandy of the Rainbow Rockets! Wow! Good kick, Sandy. On it goes, heading down field close to the goal. Off to the side! Kicked by the side kicker, Tanner. Score! Way to go team!

We played hard, had fun, and did our best the whole game. So did the Space Kickers, but the one point was the only point scored. Good game gals and guys!

After the game we all went over to the coach's house for treats. We usually have some kind of candy bar or a drink. This time we had pizza delivered. What a day! What a game!

Jorgie's Jive

It is always a good idea to go back and read stories you've already read. Also pick your favorite stories and read them to a friend or younger brother or sister.

Name _____

Follow-Up Activities for "Rainbow Rockets versus Space Kickers"

Reading Comprehension questions for discussion between child and parent/adult:

1. What do you need to protect yourself when playing soccer?
2. What are the rules for playing soccer?
3. Who do you think is the most important player? Why?
4. What does "penny flip" mean?
5. Why do you have to have a goalie? What do other games have that would be similar to a goalie?

Put the players names in alphabetical order: Jeff, Ben, Spencer, Flip, Scooter, Mandi, Sandy and Tanner

1. _____   2. _____   3. _____   4 _____

5. _____   6. _____   7. _____   8. _____

Thinking About the Story:

What do you think is the most important thing that the coach said?

What would you tell your team to do if you were the coach?

What is your favorite team sport? Why?

What do you think the Rainbow Rockets said to the Space Kickers after the game?

What would you have said to the Space Kickers?

WRITING PROMPT: Invent a new game that is played with something else besides a ball. Write down the rules for the new game. It would be fun to do a survey of friends, neighbors, and family to see what their favorite sport is.

Bird Songs

Oh, there's music
In the forests
And there's music
In the glen
As the birds
Are warbling greetings
To the spring
That's come again.
All their piping
Is so merry
That the woodlands
Seem to ring

With the praises
Of the bird songs
For the coming
Of the spring.
Join the joyous
Woodland chorus
And raise high
Your voice in cheer -
Join the bird songs
In thanksgiving
For the springtime
Of the year.

- **Anonymous**

After reading the poem do the following:

1. What are the two words in the poem that mean the same?

2. A glen is
   A. top of the hill
   B. valley off by itself
   C. mountains
   D. country

3. The poem is about
   A. the coming of spring
   B. the coming of summer
   C. the seasons
   D. time and weather

SUMMER NOTES:

Make a list of fun, interesting or exciting things you have done or want to do this summer.

Can't think of anything? Here's an idea. Go to the library and check out books about your favorite animal. Draw a picture.

Tea Time

Dear Friends,
You are invited to "Tea Time" at my house. We will have it in my backyard at 2:30pm on Thursday, June 12.

Your Friend,

Allie

Today is the big day for Tea Time with my friends! Am I ready? I think so. Let me look at my "checklist".

My Checklist
✔ Letters to friends.
✔ Buy food for party.
✔ Put up card table and chairs.
✔ Put on tablecloth, napkins and dishes.
✔ Get food ready to serve.
✔ Welcome friends and have party!

I'm almost ready. "Mom, can you help me, please?" "Sure, Allie," called mom, "I will help you with the food for your friends." "Here we have sandwiches, chips and lemonade", said mom. "I think that we are all set." "Here come my friends, Jacob, Daniel, and Sara."

"Welcome to my party. Let's get started. Come into my backyard and sit down."

We had so much fun at my party. We ate sandwiches and drank lemonade. We ate most of the chips. Afterwards, mom brought out chocolate chip cookies and ice-cream for dessert.

We played tag and hide-and-seek. Last of all we watched a video about aliens and Captain Bill, then all my friends had to go home.

Mom added one more thing to my checklist.
✔ Clean up and put everything away.

Mom helped me clean up. "Thanks mom, for helping me to have such a fun party." "You are welcome," said mom. "Love you, mom." "Love you too, Allie," said mom.

Jorgie's Jive

Are you writing in your summer journal? Make sure to keep track of all the fun things you are doing. Have you shared your journal with others?

Follow-Up Activities for "Tea Time"

Reading Comprehension questions for discussion between child and parent/adult:

1. What does "tea time" mean? What does it mean in the story?
2. Why is it a good idea to have a "checklist?"
3. Why is it a good idea to let people know ahead of time about a party?
4. What do you need to have a party? What's the most important thing on the list? Why?
5. Who do you think was in charge of the party, Allie or Mom? Why?

Put numbers by the sentences in the order of what happened.

_____ Allie and her mom buy food for the party.
_____ Got food ready to serve at party.
_____ Invitations to friends by Allie.
_____ Allie got cardtable, chairs, table cloth, napkin and dishes ready.
_____ Cleaned up and put everything away.
_____ Had refreshments, watched video, had fun and played games.

Mark the vowels in the following words as short, long, or silent

yellow	woke	shelf	rule
post	shy	sheep	fast
game	himself	instead	alphabet
what	soft	city	boat
cage	dinner	happy	grow
yet	with	tiny	street
copy	study	those	travel
nose	whales	mean	letter
over	paper	middle	expect

How many small words can you find in these words?

spend	stitch	visitor	another	scratch	rabbit
hamburger	lemonade	herself	fraction	vacation	together
started	himself	meanings	kitchen	canyon	chocolate
sister	sentence	opened	belonging	basement	snowed

WRITING PROMPT: Plan the refreshments for a party. Write an invitation for a birthday party or a family reunion.

Tulips

In my flower garden, tulips grow,

Straight like soldiers in a row.

Winds cause them to sway,

They brighten up our every day.

The shiny petals like a cup,

Drink the rain and sunshine up.

You keep blooming so bright,

You are nature's beautiful sight.

In my garden tulips grow,

Straight like soldiers in a row.

After reading the poem answer the following questions.

1. **The poem is mainly about**

    A. flowers

    B. nature

    C. tulips

    D. soldiers

2. **The tulips grow**

    A. crowded

    B. straight

    C. crooked

    D. all over

3. **"brighten up our day" means**

    A. makes us unhappy

    B. nature is beautiful

    C. makes us shine

    D. makes us happy

4. **In the poem we learn that**

    A. all kinds of flowers grow

    B. flowers and weeds grow

    C. flowers never die

    D. tulips grow

27

Bugs

"Yikes! Run Mandi, there's a bug!" yelled Jack.

"I don't run from bugs. I like bugs," Mandi said.

"You do?" asked Jack.

"My sister and I have a bug club. Come over to my house, I'll show you some of our bugs. We also have lots of books about bugs," Mandi replied.

"This jar has two grasshoppers in it. We put grass, twigs, and dead flies in the jar with them. My sister keeps them for two or three days and then we let them go so that they can survive longer," she explained.

"Let me show you our ant farm. Ants are so interesting. They like to make tunnels and pockets. They live in large groups. They all have jobs. Worker ants are the hardest workers. They get food for all the ants. They take care of the ant eggs in the nests," Mandi told Jack. "Ants can live almost anywhere. That is why there are so many."

"You sure know a lot about bugs," said Jack. "Do you know which bug makes the best mother?"

"It's the earwig," Mandi answered. "Let me show you a picture of one. She spends all winter looking after her eggs. She licks them clean and keeps them warm. When they hatch, she feeds them."

"This is a picture of a louse. She carries her babies in a pouch, just as kangaroos do! Look at this picture. It is a giraffe weevil. Guess how it got it's name?" Mandi asked. "You guessed right. It's neck is two times as long as it's body. That is how it got it's name."

"Summer is a good time to collect bugs, Jack," Mandi shouted. "Grab a jar." "Let's go see if we can catch some."

"Okay," said Jack, "this should be fun. Mandi, I'm glad that we're not afraid of bugs!"

Jorgie's Jive

I hope that you are having a good summer and that you like reading these and other stories!

Follow-Up Activities for "Bugs"

Reading Comprehension questions for discussion between child and parent/adult:
1. What do you know about bugs?
2. Did you learn something new when you read this story? What?
3. What did they put in the jar with the grasshoppers? Why?
4. Are there some bugs that Mandi and Jack are afraid of?
5. Are there some bugs that you should be afraid of? Why? Which ones?
6. What else does Mandi have besides a bug collection that's interesting?

How many words can you make out of the letters used in the word grasshoppers? You may use the letters more than once.

1. _____	2. _____	3. _____	4. _____
5. _____	6. _____	7. _____	8. _____
9. _____	10. _____	11. _____	12. _____
13. _____	14. _____	15. _____	16. _____
17. _____	18. _____	19. _____	20. _____

Homographs are words that are spelled alike but have different meaning. Use these homographs in the sentences below: park, tall, punch, rock, stand, fall.
1. When the leaves turn different colors and drop from the tree, it is _____.
2. I love to go to the _____ and play on all the play equipment.
3. Grandma likes to sit in her rocking chair and _____ back and forth.
4. Grant doubled up his fist to _____ the punching bag hard.
5. Don't throw a _____ at cars, you might break their windshield.
6. _____ up for America when you say the Pledge of Allegiance.
7. I love _____ made from lemonade, orange juice and ginger ale.
8. Make sure that when we _____ the car we take the keys out.
9. The President took the _____ and gave a great speech.
10. Children should never climb on high ladders because they could _____ and get hurt.

WRITING PROMPT: Create a new kind of bug. Give it a name. Write a description of it. Where does it live and what does it do? How do you know if it's a good bug or a dangerous bug? What does it eat? What else does it do?

29

The Flea Market

"Wake up if you want to go with us, Nellie." yelled dad. "We are going to the flea market."

I tumbled out of bed, got dressed, brushed my teeth, ate some breakfast and said, "I'm ready. What's a flea market?" Dad replied, "That's where people take things to sell and where people come to buy things." "Okay, sounds good to me," I said.

We got to the place where the flea market was. We looked all around to see what we might want to buy. "How about a dish for our fish?" I asked. "Not a dish for a fish," said mom, "but a dish for a dog, that is a dog dish." "How about a hat for the cat?" I asked. "Not a hat for a cat," laughed dad, "but a hat for Pat." "Pat would like that hat!" he yelled! I asked if we could get a rug and a wig. Mom wanted to know why. I said, "The rug is for Pug the dog. The wig is for my friend Mig to give to her mom." "Pug will not want the rug," replied dad.

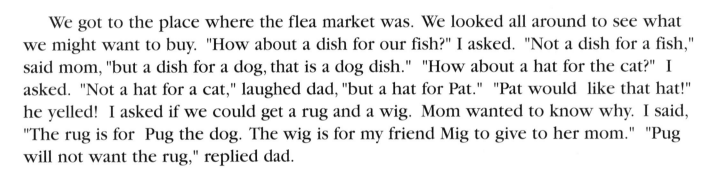

"We will get him the dog dish and Mig's mom does not need a wig. We will get Mig a big fig , not a wig," Mom said. "What other things do we need to get?" I asked. "Keep looking, we may see something else that we want but not need," said dad.

When we got home, we unpacked all the things that we bought. "We got lots of neat stuff, but I think we forgot something," I said. "What?" asked mom. "Fleas! We didn't buy any fleas at the flea market," I said. Mom and dad just giggled and said, "I don't think we need any fleas, nor do we want any!"

Jorgie's Jive

Are you reading the stories several times? Are you going back and rereading stories you've already read. Trust me, it's a good idea to do that. It's great practice for great readers!

Follow-Up Activities for "The Flea Market"

Reading Comprehension questions for discussion between child and parent/adult:

1. What's a flea market?
2. What else do you think you could buy at a flea market?
3. What time do you think they went to the flea market? Why?
4. What would you like to take to a flea market to sell? Why?
5. There are a lot of words that rhyme in the story. What makes them rhyme?
6. What's the difference between a yard sell and a flea market?

Buy and sell are words that are called opposites (antonyms). Match the opposites (antonyms). Write the matching opposites (antonyms) in the blanks using these words: sad, down, dirty, finish, close, find, before, none, cold, laugh, near, sharp, light, start, awake, common, female, summer, cheap, pull, take, rude, empty, below, go.

give _____   funny _____   male _____

dull _____   lose _____   up _____

cry _____   stop _____   far _____

hot _____   full _____   winter _____

start _____   clean _____   open _____

polite _____   dark _____   above _____

asleep _____   push _____   expensive_____

all _____   after _____

Read the story again and write the rhyming words that you find. Then add one or two more rhyming words to each pair.

WRITING PROMPT: Pretend you are at a flea market. Make a list of things that you might want to buy for each member of your family, including your pets if you have any.

OUR TREE HOUSE

My friend and I are way up high

Watching the world go by,

Up in our tree house.

Way down below on the ground

Little people move around,

While we're up in our tree house.

Birds fly above and below us

They are so noisy, making such a fuss,

They think that it's their tree house!

After Reading, do the following:

1. Reread each verse and write down the rhyming words.

2. What other things could they see on the ground besides people?

3. Why would birds make a fuss about the children?

4. Write what you think the tree house looks like, is made of, or what might be inside it.

Being A Pilot

I think that when I grow up I'd like to be a pilot. It appears to me that they lead an exciting life. Just imagine being up in the sky with the wind underneath you, holding you up, while the ground below calls for you to come back home!

I'd stay up for a long, long time, following the birds in flight. They could never keep up with me if we had a race! Silly to even think that they might.

I'd like to weave in and out among the billowing clouds like sails in the sky. I'm not too sure about storm clouds though. I think that it might be a little frightening, especially if there was lightning flashing all around. I wouldn't want to get struck by lightning anytime, let alone while I was flying! I've never really heard of a large plane being hurt by lightning. Pilots probably know all about how to handle situations like that.

Sometimes our family goes out by the airport and parks in this special spot where we can see the airplanes really well! I get excited just watching the airplanes land and take off! When we stand outside watching, the noise sometimes hurts our ears. We mostly have to shout at each other to be heard.

One time our class at school went on a field trip to the airport. We walked all around and watched people get their tickets and check their luggage. We even got to go behind to watch the luggage being loaded on small tractors, then loaded onto the planes. Last of all we got to go inside one of the large passenger jets!

I hope that someday, before too long, I get to take a ride in an airplane! I want to experience first-hand what it really feels like, so I'll know for sure if I want to be a pilot when I grow up!

Jorgie's Jive

Are you taking time to do the Reading Comprehension questions for discussion? These questions give purpose for reading. If your children cannot effectively take part in this, they probably need to spend more time with the stories.

Follow-Up Activities for "Being A Pilot"

Reading Comprehension questions for discussion between child and parent/adult:

1. What does the story tell you about clouds? Are there other kinds?
2. Can lightning be dangerous? What should you do during a lightening storm?
3. Why does the family have to shout at each other?
4. What are some things that happened at the airport?
5. What's exciting about being a pilot?

What does the underlined word mean?
Circle your answer.

1. It <u>appears</u> to me that they are hiding something.
   a. looks like   b. does not look like

2. It's <u>exciting</u> that we get to take swimming lessons.
   a. silly   b. fantastic   c. no fun

3. The airplane flew <u>beneath</u> the clouds.
   a. over   b. away from   c. under

4. Some people are <u>frightened</u> of the dark and need a nightlight.
   a. tickles   b. scared   c. not scared

5. It takes <u>several</u> people to make a family happy.
   a. none   b. some   c. everybody

6. Macie struck a home run <u>yesterday</u>.
   a. today   b. tomorrow   c. day before today

7. I don't think that <u>could</u> ever happen.
   a. might   b. never   c. forever

8. The birds took <u>flight</u> up high in the air.
   a. crawled   b. flew   c. zoomed

Fill in the blanks with spl, spr, str, thr to make real words.

ong	ay	atter
ow	it	ing
ash	eet	ead
ang	ee	ough
ay	ing	ead
int	inkle	ill
oat	ee	

WRITING PROMPT: Write about what you would like to be when you grow up. What would make it exciting or worthwhile? How could this make you happy?

35

My Grandpa and I, Part 1

My grandpa has this neat cabin in Snow Canyon that we go to sometimes. To get there, you have to go off the main road. You drive back and forth on this twisty dirt road for quite a while. Sometimes I say, "When are we ever going to get there, Grandpa?"

My grandpa just smiles and says, "Just a few more miles, Little Bud, just a few more miles."

Sometimes I take a short nap, then it doesn't seem to take so long to get there. When I wake up, I'm ready and eager. The trees, the flowers and the mountains seem like old friends.

I know we are there! The car rolls to a sluggish stop. We unpack our gear. Afterwards we walk outside. I know just what my grandpa is going to say. "Just listen," says he, "there's no sound quite like this."

With his fingers to his lips, grandpa and I just stand still. We hear the water calling us from the creek nearby. The wind is waking up the leaves. Far off, you can hear the birds singing their message to each other. I'm sure the insects are up and about, doing what I would think are their chores. Grandpa thinks so too.

After we eat the lunch grandma packed for us , we take our stroll through the woods. Grandpa says that he'll follow me this time.

We gather wild daisies, sunflowers, bluebonnets and our Indian paint brush. We greet the new little pine trees and check the growth of the quaking aspen trees. Some trees have fallen from the winter snow, resting for a time before joining the forest floor.

I put my hand in grandpa's.

"Yes, Little Bud, I think it's time," says grandpa.

We go back to the cabin, grab our fishing poles and race each other to the creek. The contest begins! "I hope I catch the most fish," I shout!

"Okay," grandpa giggles, "but it's my turn to catch the biggest!"

Jorgie's Jive

Do you have a library card or do you already have lots of books to read at your house?

Follow-Up Activities for "Grandpa and Me" part 1

Reading Comprehension questions for discussion between child and parent/adult:
1. What do you think "the flowers and mountains seem like old friends" means?
2. What was Grandpa saying when he said, "Just listen, there's no sound quite like this"?
3. What were the birds doing in the story?
4. What happens to trees when they fall over in the forest?
5. What do you think live in the creek by Grandpa's cabin? Anything else?

Put numbers on the sentences the in order that they happened.

_____ I took a short nap so that when I woke up I would be ready for whatever happened

_____ I can hear the wind, the water and the birds singing to each other.

_____ The car rolled to a sluggish stop.

_____ We went fishing and the contest began!

_____ We went for a walk through the woods and gathered wild flowers.

_____ We ate lunch.

_____ We grabbed our fishing poles and raced to the creek.

Combine the following words with those listed below to make compound words: pole, foot, flies, room, time, ball, truck, cake, light, fork, stand, hook, fork, yard, box, corn, shine, book, bath, bow.

butter _____	bed _____	pan _____	barn _____
fire _____	bare _____	rain _____	pop _____
pitch _____	spring _____	fish _____	cook _____
lunch _____	flag _____	bird _____	under _____
foot _____	sun _____	mail _____	star _____

Write some of your own endings to make these words into compound words.

book _____   finger _____   down _____   rain _____

WRITING PROMPT: Make a list of things that you would take with you if you went fishing with someone. Make a picture of you fishing and where you went fishing (creek, river, ocean, lake, pond).

Let's Go!

Our family had been saving up for a trip! It took a long time to save enough to go but we finally did!

My sister delivered newspapers around the neighborhood. She saved at least half of her money to put in the "family trip money jar". I took my uncle's dog for a walk almost every day. He paid me fifty cents every time I did. Most of my money went into our money jar, too.

Instead of fixing so many desserts for dinner, mom saved that money and put it aside for our trip. Dad helped too, by taking his lunch to work instead of eating out for lunch.

We recycled our aluminum cans. After we saved many cans, we took them to the recycling place. They gave us money for the cans we had.

We had family meetings. We checked our trip account frequently to see how we were doing. Last week when we met, we decided that we probably had enough money! We discussed some of the places we might be able to go. We talked about camping, flying to grandma and grandpa Hanson's house in Florida, going to California to Disneyland, to the ocean or to Washington D.C.!

After thinking and talking about it for some time we finally decided. We decided that if we drove to grandpa's and grandma's house, we would be able to stay with them longer. We could probably go to Disney World while we were there.

We packed our suitcases and put them in the car. We put a few of our toys and games in so that we would have something to do along the way. We also packed our journals so we could keep track of the interesting things we saw and did.

Mom packed a lunch for us to eat the first day. She also packed a few extra cookies and potato chips for snacks. We filled empty plastic bottles with ice-water to drink.

My dad checked the car carefully. He checked the oil and filled the car with gas. He grabbed a map and said, "Okay everyone, are we ready?"

We were! We took one last look around to make sure that we didn't forget anything important. We turned off the lights and locked the doors. We said good-bye to our neighbors.

Dad honked the horn one last time as we all climbed in. "Destination grandma's and grandpa's house," we all yelled!

Follow-Up Activities for "Let's Go"

Reading Comprehension questions for discussion between child and parent/adult:

1. How long do you think it probably took the family to get to Florida? Why?
2. Do you think this family had a lot of money, some money or very little money? Why?
3. How did they get enough money to go on the trip?
4. How else do you think they could get money to go?
5. What happened at their family meetings? Do you think that they had a lot of meetings or a few? Why?

Write in the missing vowels to make real words.

dr _ _ m   c _ _ nt   tr _ _ n   r _ _ nb _ w   gr _ _ n

ag _ _ n   g _ _ng   cr _ wl _ ng   pl _ c _   gr _ _ t

_ n _ m _ l   p _ nn _

Use the words above to complete these sentences.

1. I could watch that video over _____, it was so good.
2. I told mom that I was _____ outside to play.
3. Mike wants me to go over to his _____ to play.
4. My favorite _____ is a playful puppy.
5. We went _____ on our hands and knees through the tunnel.
6. I found a shiny _____ on my way to school.
7. I think the color _____ belongs to spring.
8. I love a rainy day because it can bring a _____.
9. I'm going to _____ the money in my piggy bank.
10. I like to ride on an Amtrack _____ to Boston.
11. I think that my mom and dad are _____ parents.
12. My favorite _____ is when I'm riding a horse.

WRITING PROMPT: Write a list of other ways that a person, kids and adults can earn and save money.

Thirty Days Has September

Thirty days has September,

April, June and November.

When short February's done,

All the rest have thirty-one.

After reading the poem do the following: List all twelve months of the year, then go back and write how many days each month has from the information given in the poem.

1. _____   7. _____

2. _____   8. _____

3. _____   9. _____

4. _____   10. _____

5. _____   11. _____

6. _____   12. _____

40

SUMMER NOTES:

Make a list of fun, interesting or exciting things you have done or want to do this summer.

Having trouble? Read the newspaper with your mom or dad. Talk about any interesting stories you may find. Have you ever thought about being a newspaper reporter?

My Grandpa and I, Part 2

Down at the creek with fishing poles in hand and worms on the hooks, grandpa and I were ready to fish! We had already scouted out the best fishing hole from other times we had fished together. Grandpa watched as I tossed my line out into the water, then he put his in. Neither one of us talked much. We just enjoyed the quiet and watched our lines.

I felt just a slight nibble on my hook. I pulled the line just a little tiny bit and then waited. This time the nibble became a bite! I jerked harder on my line and began reeling in the fish! I kept reeling and the fish kept fighting.

"Hang in there, Little Bud." said Grandpa, "It looks like a good one!"

It didn't take long before I had the fish out and into my fishing box. It was a rainbow trout, one of my favorite kind to eat. I grinned over at my grandpa just as his line took a strong jerk. Grandpa let out a short squeal! It was his turn to bring in a fish.

After a while grandpa caught another one. I hadn't yet. We decided to move down the creek a ways to try our luck there. We caught a few more and kept moving slowly down to more spots along the creek, fishing as we went.

My grandpa and I always have such a good time together. I got my hook stuck a couple of times. Grandpa helped me get it unstuck and back into the water.

It started to get late, so we went back to the cabin. We cleaned and counted the fish. I caught the most! I caught seven real good ones. Grandpa only caught five but he did catch the biggest one!

That night we ate fried fish and dutch oven potatoes. We drank water from the creek and roasted marshmallows on a stick on the campfire. We decided that we'd take our sleeping bags outside and sleep under the stars!

My grandpa hugged me good night and said, "This is the perfect ending for a perfect day together!" I smiled in agreement just before nodding off to sleep.

My Grandpa's Dutch-Oven Potatoes:

Grandpa makes his Dutch-Oven Potatoes in a "Dutch-Oven" pan, which is a heavy cast-iron pan with a lid to match. He puts bacon, onions, and potatoes inside. Sometimes grandpa adds a can of cream of mushroom soup.

The best part of my grandpa's recipe is how he cooks it. First he digs a hole in the ground. Then he covers the pan with it's lid. Next he buries the pan in the ground with coals from our campfire!

The potatoes cook for 2 hours underground. When we're ready to eat, grandpa digs up the pan, brushes off the dirt, and serves me steaming hot Dutch Oven Potatoes. They taste great!

Follow-Up Activities for "Grandpa and Me" part 2

Reading Comprehension questions for discussion between child and parent/adult:

1. How did Little Bud and his grandpa know where to fish?
2. Do you think Little Bud is the boy's real name? Why or Why not?
3. What does a fisherman usually do when he feels a slight nibble on his line?
4. From this story, what do you know about fishing along a creek?
5. How many fish did each of them catch? How many in all?

Check the two sentences that have something to do with the story.

_____ Grandpa squealed and Little Bud grinned because they were having such a good time fishing.

_____ Grandpa and Little Bud walked a long, long time and grew tired and weary, so they stopped to rest and fish.

_____ Grandpa and Little Bud probably cooked their fish in a large frying pan outside on the fire.

Write in the correct part of the word for each sentence.

1. Sam will r____ the wild horse.
   ide ake
2. "Mother, can you find the b___ for me?"
   oll all
3. Ralph and Nancy w___ to the grocery store. ent ant
4. "I'm not worried, Tom knows his w___ there." ith ay
5. Aunt Ellen does not live very f___ away.
   ar or
6. "I have the paint and brush so let's paint the d___." ack eck

Write some rhyming words to go with the following words:

dish   while   creek   slight   try

_____   _____   _____   _____   _____

_____   _____   _____   _____   _____

WRITING PROMPT: Write about a perfect day, or write about a day when everything seemed to go wrong. It can a real or a make-believe story.

Dream Party

Next week is my birthday! Our family celebrates birthdays by having family parties. I get to choose my favorites for dinner. I want pepperoni pizza, salad, breadsticks and dip. I want soda pop to drink, and of course we can't forget a birthday cake with ice cream! Afterwards I get to choose a video to watch, or choose my favorite family game to play. I haven't decided yet whether to watch a video or to play Monopoly.

That night when I went to bed, I had been thinking about my birthday. I had this wild and wacky dream! In my dream I had an awesome party. It all started when a truck carrying a hot air ballon pulled up in front of our house!

The driver set up in our front yard. When it was all ready, my friends and I stepped in for a ride. We went almost straight up! We flew over house tops, over tall skyscrapers and over mountains. Everything looked so small. People were no bigger than ants crawling on the ground. The cars looked like toy match-box cars. The houses looked like they belonged to some kind of doll.

The wind helped by blowing us along so fast! We went out over the ocean. It made my friend, Jude a little seasick or maybe it's called airsick. I'm not sure.

There were seagulls flying just under us. They looked so graceful that for awhile it seemed as if I was flying right with them.

We flew on and on, higher and higher. The earth began growing smaller and smaller as we moved on. The stars and moon joined us. That's when I decided that it was getting late and we needed to get back in time for refreshments before everyone had to go home.

I went looking for the owner to ask him to take us back. I couldn't find him anywhere. My friends said that they couldn't remember seeing him after we left the ground.

"Oh, no! We were on our own!" I thought. None of us knew how to operate a hot-air balloon! We knew if we didn't do things right we could crash! About that time a helicopter came close to us! We all hollered as loud as we could, "Help, help us please!" We kept screaming that we needed help, as the helicopter went on it's merry way, without paying any attention to us!

The next thing I knew, I was being shaken several times. It was then that I woke up! My parents said that I kept hollering in my sleep for help. They wanted to know if there was something that they could do for me. I said, "No, you already have! You got us all safely back to earth and into our own bedrooms!"

"Man, that must have been some dream!" my father said.

"Believe me," I laughed, "It was some birthday!"

Jorgie's Jive

Have you kept a list of your favorite stories? It would be fun to share your list with a friend.

Follow-Up Activities for "Dream Party"

Reading Comprehension questions for discussion between child and parent/adult:

1. The first part of the story talks about what kind of birthday party?
2. What does "wild and wacky "mean to you? What does it mean in the story?
3. What did the children see while they were in the hot - air balloon?
4. What other types of transportation could have given the children a "wild and wacky" ride?
5. How else could this story have ended?
6. Could this birthday dream really happen?

Categorize the following into two or three different groups. You decide where they should go. Tell an adult why you grouped them that way. There are no wrong answers because this is your choice of grouping.

house tops, skyscrapers, mountains, ants, doll houses, ocean, sea gulls, hot-air balloon, helicopter, stars, moon, and clouds

Choose the correct word that goes in the following sentences.

1. Riley and I _____ a lot of people we knew. see   saw   seen
2. I fell down when I was running and _____ my shirt. tear   tore   torn
3. Grandma and I have _____ letters to each other. write   wrote   written
4. I felt bad when I did something wrong because I _____ better. knew   know   known
5. We had _____ a long way in the car before we stopped. ride   rode   ridden
6. My grandpa said that I have _____ a lot since last year. grew   grow   grown
7. We had to _____ the ice cream again because it had melted. freeze   froze   frozen
8. The phone _____ over and over before I answered it. rung   rang   ring

WRITING PROMPT: Have you ever had a "wild and wacky" dream? If so write about it, or write about your favorite birthday.

45

Come to the Meadow

Come to the meadow where the prim rose grows,

Buttercups looking as yellow as gold.

Daisies and cowslips beginning to bloom.

`Tis a beautiful sight to behold.

Busy bees humming about them are seen,

Butterflies happily fluttering along.

Grasshoppers chirp in the hedges so green,

Linnet is singing his liveliest song.

After reading the poem do the following:

Name two or three other bugs or insects you would find in a meadow.
1.
2.
3.

Name two or three other kinds of flowers you would find in a meadow.
1.
2.
3.

In line 5 the word "them" refers to what?

Look in the dictionary to find the countries where the Linnet lives.

Name _____

Little brown seeds placed in the ground,

Grow with rain and sunshine.

Secretly they seem to grow,

Impatiently I wait to see them.

Then one morning they peek through,

Life around them is green.

Beautiful flowers we come to know,

Were little brown seeds we knew.

After reading the poem do the following:

1. Name different kinds of seeds you might want to plant.

2. In the third line of the poem what does the word "they" mean?

3. What other plants have seeds?

4. What does the last line of the poem mean?

A Walk On The Farm

We went to visit Uncle Rick and Aunt Mable. They live on a farm. After lunch, my Aunt and Uncle invited us to go for a walk around the farm.

In the barn we saw two horses, Nip and Tuck. They each had a baby foal. The foals didn't have names yet. My little brother, Jason said they should be called Rip and Luck.

Aunt Mable replied, "My, my, Nip and Rip, Tuck and Luck."

"That sounds pretty good don't you think," said Jason.

"Maybe so," laughed Uncle Rick.

Three cows also live in the barn. Uncle Rick has to milk them in the morning and again at night. Five Nanny goats bang around in the barn, too.

"Now what do you do with Nanny goats?" my Dad asked.

Aunt Mable informed us that some people give their babies goat's milk instead because they are allergic to cow's milk.

"Wow," I thought to myself, "it must get awfully crowded in the barn, four horses, three cows and five Nanny goats." My little brother says that he wants to live in the barn with all the animals! He is only three years old. Mom told him that he would have to grow a lot older before she would even think about it.

Next we stopped by the pig pen. The mother sow just had a litter of pigs. There were ten little piglets. They were tiny and pinkish. I wanted to play with one but my uncle said that the mother pig would get really upset if she couldn't see all ten of her babies. I was impressed to think that pigs could count, well mother pigs anyway!

We helped gather the eggs in the chicken coop. We gathered mostly white eggs. There were just a few brown ones. I wanted to know if they were chocolate flavored eggs. My mom laughed at that question and dad explained that white eggs and brown eggs are the same inside. I wondered if there were other colors of chicken eggs but I didn't ask.

We had to leave to go home before we got to see all the animals. My aunt and uncle said that we would have to come again soon. They suggested that next time maybe we could stay overnight so that we could see more of the farm. "Maybe next time you could even help milk the cows and feed the animals," they said. I can hardly wait!

Follow-Up Activities for "A Walk On The Farm"

Reading Comprehension questions for discussion between child and parent/adult:

1. What did the children see on the farm?
2. They didn't get to see all the animals. Which ones do you think they missed?
3. What do you think "litter of pigs" means?
4. Where would you find different colored eggs than the ones talked about in the story?
5. The children wanted to help feed the animals. What do you think they eat?

Use the correct homonym in the following sentences.

1. I fell down the stairs and got a _____ on my head.   not   knot
2. When we went for a drive, I saw a _____.   dear   deer
3. We ran all around the park and I _____ everyone!   beat   beet
4. My dad said, "Well _____ , I think we'd better go.   sun   son
5. I _____ like to ride on all the rides at Disneyland.   wood   would
6. One, two, three, _____ buttons are on my blouse.   for   four   fore
7. I'd like a big _____ of chocolate cake for dessert.   piece   peace
8. I went over _____ my friend's house yesterday.   to   too   two

Palindromes are words that read the same backwards and forwards.

deed   noon   sis   eye   level
ewe   pup   rotor   reviver   gag

These words change when you read them forward and backward.

step   pals   warts   trap   wolf   loots
raw   tort   part

See if you can write some palindromes and some words that change when you read them forward and backward.

Write a definition for:
homonym _____

WRITING PROMPT: Write about some of your relatives and where they live. What do they do? What would you do if you went there for a visit?

Sing a Song of Summer

Summer opened her heart up wide,

I looked in to see the sky so blue.

I grabbed my cap and rushed outside,

The sun was there to greet me, too.

The butterflies were flying,

Meadowlarks kept singing.

Mother animals watched babies trying,

With spindly, wobbly legs winging.

Hold on to summer while you can,

Fall will swiftly come along.

Gather treasures in a large pan,

Build summer memories for your own song.

After reading the poem do the following:

1. What do you think the first line of the poem means?

    A.   a box full of surprises.

    B.   Fall is almost here.

    C.   Summer is really here.

    D.   a mystery box.

2. What do the words "box" and "pan" mean in the poem?

    A.   real boxes and pans

    B.   air

    C.   nothing

    D.   containers

3. What does "the sun was there to greet me!" mean?

4. What summer memories could you put in your own box or pan?

Back To The Farm

Dear Jason and Brett,

We loved having you visit us the other day. You just didn't stay long enough for us. You are invited to come back to the farm to stay a few days. Please ask your parents if you can come soon. If your parents want to bring you out, we could take you home. Maybe your folks could stay overnight and go home the next day.

Your cousins, Alex and Ellie, want to come, too. We thought that it would be fun if you could come at the same time. It would be like having a farm party with all of you here!

Please write us a letter or call us on the phone to let us know if you can come.
Love,
Uncle Rick & Aunt Mable

Arrangements were made and we all arrived at the farm late at night. Our parents left the next day.

We woke up kind of late. Aunt Mable fixed us a huge country-style breakfast. We had ham and eggs, hash browns, pancakes, orange juice and milk. We were so full that we practically waddled away from the table. Uncle Rick said that he had a big day ahead of him. We followed him out the door asking if we could come too. We thought that maybe we could help.

He said,"I have some neighbors coming to help cut and haul hay. I'll tell you what," he said, "I'll take two of you with me today, then two of you tomorrow. Two can help me and two can help Aunt Mable. Two at a time, that will work out just right."

We watched the helpers cut and chop the hay in the field. Uncle Rick told us that it was the second cutting of hay and that it was a good second crop. He also told us that they leave it out in the field for a few days to dry, while they bring in the other fields that are ready. We got to ride on the tractor with the loader to pick up the bales and put them on the big trailer. Uncle Rick even let us steer the tractor just a little! We followed the big truck and trailer in and watched as the helpers unloaded and stacked it.

That night, Uncle Rick and Aunt Mable talked about when they were little. They said that cutting and stacking the hay was much different then. Workers cut the hay without baling it. The hay was just loose. After it was cut they used big forks called pitchforks to pick it up and load it on the wagons.

They told us it was much more work then than it is now. They added that it was a lot more fun because the children loved to climb on the haystacks and slide down them!

Follow-Up Activities for "Back To The Farm"

Reading Comprehension questions for discussion between child and parent/adult:

1. How many people are mentioned in the story? Can you name them?
2. What does it mean when it said "arrangements were made"?
3. Why do you think Uncle Rick took two children with him and left two behind for the next day?
4. What are the many things a farmer does with hay?
5. Can you name some of the things that were different years ago on the farm and the way it is now?

Read the sentences and decide whether they are real or make-believe. Write r if they are real and mb if they are make-believe.

1. People live in houses made of bricks, wood and clay. _____
2. Mother pigs count their baby pigs to keep track of them. _____
3. Fall leaves can be any color, size and shape. _____
4. All birds are alike in some ways and different in others. _____

Read the words starting with the letter "g;" they have soft sounds, and hard sounds, and some are silent: gerbil   garbage giant   gnaw   sign   guest   goose   gnarled
      Now use the words above in these sentences.

1. A beaver has very sharp teeth so that it can _____ and cut wood.
2. The gander and the _____ are feathered friends.
3. My _____ is a friendly and cuddly pet that loves to run.
4. We put a "For Sale" _____ on my old bike because it was too small for me.
5. The old tree was bent, twisted and _____.
6. My brother and I take out the _____ twice a day.
7. We have a _____ coming for dinner.
8. The _____ roared, "Fee, Fi, Fo, Fum."

WRITING PROMPT: Write about why farmers are so important to us. Or you could write about what you would like to do if you were a farmer.

Helping Aunt Mable

Today Jason and Ellie went with Uncle Rick. Alex and I stayed with Aunt Mable.

After breakfast we helped with the dishes. Aunt Mable said, "Okay boys, our tummies are full, now we need to go feed the animals so that their tummies are full. When Uncle Rick is not working in the hay he helps feed the animals but now we need to do his part."

We fed the chickens and ducks some corn. We gathered the eggs from the chicken coop, then we stopped by the pigpen. We gave the pigs all the leftovers that Aunt Mable had when she cleaned out her refrigerator. We fed them some grain and water,

too. The next animals on our list were the animals in the barn. We put a new block of salt out for the cows. We gave the horses and cows some hay and grain. We refilled the water troughs with clean water. We let the goats out in the pasture so they could nibble on fresh grass and drink from the pond.

We watched Aunt Mable wash and sterilize the milking machines that Uncle Rick had used to milk the cows and goats earlier. We gave some of the milk to the two cats that were in the barn, as well as some canned cat food.

As we walked back toward the farmhouse, we were met by barks from Sandy. He wanted something to eat, too. He probably thought that we had forgotten him. We scratched him behind his ears and told him that he was next. We put some dry dogfood in his dish along with some warm water and stirred it around a little. We put fresh water in his other dish. We told him that he could have some dog biscuits later.

We had a little time to play before lunch. We swung on the tire swing on the big old maple tree in the back yard.

After lunch we went back out to the barn. We let the cows and horses out in the pasture by the barn so that we could clean out the stalls in the barn. We had to put fresh straw on the barn floor for the animals. It took us quite a while to get all this done.

We helped wash and hang clothes out on the clothesline to dry. Aunt Mable told us that she likes to dry the clothes on the line outside. She likes the way they smell when she brings them back in.

After dinner that night, while Uncle Rich was milking the goats and cows, we popped popcorn and chose a video to watch! When Uncle Rich came in, we ate popcorn, drank home-made root beer and watched videos. Jason and Ellie fell asleep on the couch. After the videos, no one had to tell us twice to go to bed. We were ready. We were tired but happy. We were anxious for another big day on the farm tomorrow!

Follow-Up Activities for "Helping Aunt Mable"

Reading Comprehension questions for discussion between child and parent/adult:

1. What do farm animals need to survive?
2. What job on the farm do you think is the hardest?
3. What job on the farm do you think is the most important?
4. What did Aunt Mable do to the milking machine? Why?
5. Can you list the many chores the boys helped with and the ones they didn't?
6. What was the chore that was done last that was almost the exact same?

Finish these sentences:

1. I could fly if I had _____
2. I could race if I had _____
3. I could grow if I had _____
4. I could laugh if I had _____
5. I could cry if I had _____
6. I could jump if I had _____
7. I could ride if I had _____
8. I could think if I had _____
9. I could swim if I had _____
10. I could draw if I had _____

Mark the silent letter/letters in these words:

weight	thumb	sign
knack	column	fence
plumber	island	whistle
written	straight	knit
neighbor	kitchen	flake

Change the last letter and add a correct ending such as "ing," "ie," "ily," "ies," "ied," "iest," for these words:

fry	_____	happy	_____	easy	_____
carry	_____	funny	_____	cry	_____
story	_____	noisy	_____	family	_____
party	_____	memory	_____	bury	

Writing Prompt: Write about the chores or responsibilities that you have. You could also write about things that need to be done around your house, inside or outside.

The Wind

It made a rustling sound

As softly through the leaves it blew,

But now it roughly swirls around

and seems to sing, "Yoo, Hoo."

After reading the poem do the following:
Write action or sound words for the wind.

1.   5.
2.   6.
3.   7.
4.   8.

Throughout the poem, what does the word "it" refer to?

What good is the wind?

Write and illustrate another verse for the poem.

SUMMER NOTES:

Make a list of your five favorites stories in this book, then write a sentence which tells why you liked them.

Do any of the stories remind you of places you'd like to visit? For example if you'd like to ride in a hot air ballon, then maybe "Dream Party," was your favorite story!

Answer Sheets

1. **Jake and the Pet Store:** Comprehension answers will vary.
   Puppy - friendly, Mouse - running, Goldfish - bubbles, Cat - playing, Gerbils - sleepy
   List of Animals will Vary.
   Word Endings: spot, spots spotting, spotted. clean, cleans, cleaning, cleaned. laugh, laughs, laughing, laughed. cover, covers, covering, covered. swim, swims, swimming. exercise, exercises, exercising. run, runs, running. blow, blows, blowing. choose, chooses, choosing.
   Fill in the Blanks: playing, run, sleep, swimming, spotted.

2. **My Home:** Comprehension answers will vary.
   Rooms: living room - couch, chairs, rugs, lamps, pictures
   Sister's bedroom - a bed, pillows, dolls, off limits sign
   boy's bedroom - toys, games, bunk beds, books
   kitchen - chairs, stove, table, refrigerator
   family room - television, computer, some games
   Vowels: not - note, cap - cape, kit - kite, red - read, bot - boat, her - here or hear, bet - beet or beat, ran - rain or roan, pop - pope, rod - rode or road, hug - huge, last - least
   True or False: T, F, F, T, T, T

3. **The Park:** Comprehension Answers will vary.
   More than one: swings, slides, lots, times, two, sandpiles, cars, tunnels, houses, mountains, trucks, rocks, kites
   Rule: When you add the "s" to words they usually mean more than one.
   Scrambled Words: unafraid, firefighter, right, emergency, astronauts, dentist, scare, crying

4. **The Library:** D, C, B. Answers will vary here.

5. **The Pond In The Jungle:** Comprehension Answers will vary.
   Verbs: is, live, said, waded, came, are, jumped, swung, dropped, comes, listen, say, rolled, hissed, slithered, hopped, were, padded, roared, sprang, popped, hungry, snapped, splashed, crashed, sprang.
   Punctuation: . ! ? ?
   Spelling: correct - knot, spoil, circus, alligators, right, already, stove, attention, slithered, pancakes, vacation, station, twinkled, careful.
   Spelling Incorrect - speel, maed, applcake, crashied, breekfast, sandwich, biking, penmenship, carful, shoees, underlined, tertles.

6. **The Lost Wheel:** Comprehension Answers will vary.
   Compound Words: somewhere, anywhere, backyard, schoolroom, playground, schoolyard, workroom, toolbox, bedroom, bathtub, mailbox, doghouse.
   Pets: dog, bird, cat
   Real Words: sand canyon decide empty drink copy change business crowd believe bottom garden glide island float ice or ace finally horse faint idea family happen kitchen join important figure hungry moment noise million listen parent order myself

7. **Dreams:** Comprehension Answers will vary.
   Replace Words will Vary
   Contractions: can't it'll we're that's you'll she's they're shouldn't hadn't they'll doesn't she'll wouldn't wasn't he's hasn't don't I'll we'll aren't I'm It's

8. **Rainbow Rockets Versus Space Kickers:** Comprehension Answers will vary.
   Alphabetical Order: Ben Flip Jeff Mandi Sandy Scooter Spencer Tanner
   Thinking About the Story: answers will vary

9. **Bird Songs:** forest, woodlands;   B; A

10. **Tea Time:** Comprehension Answers will vary.
    Sequence: 2, 4, 1, 3, 6, 5
    Mark Vowels: yellow woke shelf rule post shy sheep fast game himself instead alphabet what soft city boat cage dinner happy grow yet with tiny street copy study those travel nose whales mean letter over paper middle expect
    Small Words in Large Words: spend stitch visitor another scratch rabbit hamburger lemonade herself fraction vacation together started himself meanings kitchen canyon chocolate sister sentences opened belonging basement snowed

11. **Tulips:** C B D D

12. **Bugs:** Comprehension Answers will vary.
    Words in Grasshoppers Will Vary: grass hopper hoppers hop pop ear ears as has so poor her hers grasp rasp reap reapers shop shape prop props grope rope ropes Pope grapes ropers
    Homographs: fall, park, rock, punch, rock, stand, punch, park, stand, fall

59

Answer Sheets

13. **The Flea Market:** Comprehension Answers will vary.
Opposites (antonyms): give - take, funny - sad, male - female, dull - sharp, lose - find, up - down, cry - laugh, stop - go, far - near, hot - cold, full - empty, winter - summer, start - finish, clean - dirty, open - close, polite - rude, dark - light, asleep - awake, push - pull, expensive - cheap, all - none, after - before, above - below
Rhyming Words: dish - fish, hat - cat - Pat, rug - Pug, wig - Mig

14. **Our Tree House:** high - by, ground - around, us - fuss. **Answers will vary.**

15. **Being A Pilot:** Comprehension Answers will vary.
Word Meanings: appears - looks like, exciting - fantastic, beneath - under, frightened - scared, several - some, yesterday - day before today, could - might, flight - flew
Fill in the Blanks: some answers may vary
strong, spray, splatter, throw, split, spring, splash, street, thread, sprang, spree, through, stray, string, spread, splint, sprinkle, thrill, throat, three

16. **Grandpa and Me part 1:** Reading Comprehension answers will vary.
Sequence of Events: 1, 3, 2, 7, 5, 4, 6
Compound Words: butterflies, bedroom, pancake, barnyard, firetruck, bare foot, rainbow, popcorn, pitchfork, springtime, fishhook, cookbook, lunchbox, flagpole, birdbath, understand, football, sunshine, mailbox, starfish
Answers will Vary: bookcase, bookworm, fingernail, fingerbowl, downstairs, downpour, rainbow, rainstorm, raindrop

17. **Let's Go:** Reading Comprehension answers will vary.
Missing Vowels: dream, count, train, rainbow, green, again, going, crawling, place, great, animal, penny
Complete the Sentences: again, going, place, animal, crawling, penny, green, rainbow, count, train, great, dream

18. **Thirty Days Has September:** January - 31, February - 28 or 29, March - 31, April - 30, May - 31, June - 30, July - 31, August - 31, September - 30, October - 31, November - 30, December - 31.

19. **My Grandpa and Me part 2:** Reading Comprehension answers will vary.
Sentences checked should be the 1st and 3rd.
Correct Part of the Word: ride, ball, went, way, far, deck
Rhyming Words: answers may vary; dish, fish, wish, swish while, mile, tile, bile, file, pile, creek, week, seek, meek, peek, cheek, slight, light, right, fight, might, sight, tight

20. **Dream Party:** Reading Comprehension answers will vary.
Categorizing: answers will vary. There are no wrong answers with this as long as the child can explain why he grouped the words together his way.
Correct words: saw, tore, written, knew, ridden, grown, freeze, rang

21. **Come to the Meadow:** #1 and #2 Answers will vary
daisies, cowslips, (buttercups, prim roses)
Africa, Europe, Asia

22. **Seeds:** #1 , #3 and #4 answers will vary, #2 they refers to plants or seeds

23. **A Walk On The Farm:** Reading Comprehension answers will vary.
Homonyms: knot, deer, beat, son, would, four, piece, to
Definition of Homonym: two or more words that are pronounced the same but are spelled differently and have different meanings.
Words will vary.

24. **Sing a Song of Summer:** C D   Answers will vary.

24. **Back To The Farm:** Reading Comprehension answers will vary.
Real or Make-Believe: r, mb, mb, r
Words in Sentences: gnaw, goose, gerbil, sign, gnarled, garbage, guest, giant

25. **Helping Aunt Mable:** Reading Comprehension answers will vary.
Finish the Sentences will Also Vary.
Silent Letters: weight thumb sign knack column fence plumber island whistle written straight knit neighbor kitchen flake
Change Letters: answers may vary
fry - fries happy - happier easy - easiest carry - carrier funny - funniest cry - cries story - stories noisy - noisiest family -families party - parties memory - memories bury - buries

26. **The Wind:** Answers will vary except for #2 - it refers to the wind

SUMMER JOURNAL:

Keep a daily journal describing your summer days on these pages.
You can also write a story about your favorite day. Have fun!

_____

_____

_____

_____

_____

_____

_____

_____

_____

_____

_____

_____

_____

_____

_____

_____

_____

 Thanks for sharing your summer with me! I hope you had a great one! Do your best in school, learning is important.

See you next year, JORGIE

Certificate of Completion

Awarded to

Name

"My brain is bigger now that I have completed Summer Bridge Reading Activities!"

George Starks

George Starks, Creative Director

Parent's Signature